M000197833

WINNING YOUR SOUTHERN CALIFORNIA DIVORCE

SPLIT DECISIONS

JOHN A. BLEDSOE
ATTORNEY AT LAW

THE BLEDSOE FIRM | LAW OFFICES OF JOHN A. BLEDSOE

(949) 363-5551
www.justfamilylaw.com

Copyright © 2020 by John A. Bledsoe

All rights reserved. No part of this book may be used or reproduced in any manner whatsoever without written permission of the author. Printed in the United States of America.

ISBN: 978-1-63385-380-5

Designed and published by
Word Association Publishers

205 Fifth Avenue
Tarentum, Pennsylvania 15084
www.wordassociation.com
1.800.827.7903

The law firm publisher makes this book available for educational purposes only.

Although this publication contains information to give you a general understanding of the topic, it does not provide legal advice. By reading this book, you understand that there is no attorney-client relationship between you and the author. This book should not be used as a substitute for competent legal advice from a licensed professional attorney in your state.

Contents

Introduction

"It is not the will to win that matters — everyone has that. It is the will to prepare to win that matters."

> - **Vince Lombardi,** *legendary football coach of the Green Bay Packers*

You have come to the right place to get information about how to win your impending divorce. There is a way to get through this process successfully. By taking the actions described here, you will not only be OK — you will win. Further, you will know how to help others who find themselves in the same situation.

My name is John A. Bledsoe. I am a seasoned family law trial attorney with over 25 years experience, and the California State Bar has designated me as a Certified Family Law Specialist.

Over two decades ago, I got my start in family law working for a charity helping low income single mothers navigate the family court system. Today my firm's clientele is far more diverse. We serve business owners, fathers, mothers, and men and women of all ages — from millennials to baby boomers to the elderly. We help people of all income levels, from working people and military members to entrepreneurs and professionals. We tackle some of Orange County's toughest divorce and family law cases, such as those involving large assets or complex custody issues. Although my clientele has diversified (somewhere along the way I had to pay back my law school tuition and raise six children), my passion for helping people has never wavered.

Since my team can't help everyone, however, I decided to write a book. These pages contain decades of family law experience distilled into practical, easy-to-understand tips.

Be forewarned — not everything I advise within these pages is "politically correct." Some may find some of my advice offensive; others may protest that the family court system isn't fair. Family law court is not always a court of fairness or even justice. Nevertheless, this is the arena that exists for everyone, so you must make the best of it.

You have a choice today. If you are facing a divorce or custody case, this may be one of the worst times in your life. You can wallow in self-pity, or you can roll up your sleeves and arm yourself with wisdom so you can fight for the best outcome possible for you and your children.

Ready? Let's get started.

chapter one
What It Means to "Win" Your Divorce Case

Smart litigants choose to put their own children through college – not their attorney's children.

Winners set smart goals and end the process as soon as possible. Losers get trapped fighting an endless court battle.

Before you start your case or file your initial response, sit down with your attorney and decide what you really need and want out of the case.

If it has already been decided that you must end your marriage, decide what you need. Examples include:

1. I need my children to have their primary residence in my home.

2. I need my one-half share of the community property.

3. I need to stay in the family residence, as I think it is best for the children.

4. I need to have a social life.

5. I need my children to be affected as little as possible, and to be emotionally healthy when this divorce is over.

6. I may be angry with my spouse, but when it's over we will need a civil working relationship so we can effectively raise our children in our separate homes.

Focus on what you absolutely need and be prepared to end the battle when you've achieved those things, or as close as your situation allows. Then — end the fight.

Don't be like King Pyrrhus

King Pyrrhus of Epirus defeated the Roman army twice — once in the battle of Heraclea in 280 BC, and again in the Battle of Asculum in 279 BC. Despite having "won," however, the cost and the casualties sustained were so high that the victories amounted to defeats for King Pyrrhus. His "wins" destroyed his kingdom and his army. To this day, when someone achieves a symbolic victory at a ruinous cost, it is known as a "pyrrhic victory."

In divorce, the parties are often aggrieved, heartbroken and even vengeful. However, with the lives of children and families at stake, the siren song of a pyrrhic victory must be avoided. If you let your aggrieved emotions lead the process — you'll end up like King Pyrrhus — with a ruined family and a drained bank account.

Winning means getting what you came for, not making the other party lose

Decide early on (before you begin dissolving your marriage) what outcomes you need to achieve to consider your case a "win." Remember — winning is accomplishing your goals, not destroying your spouse. It is about negotiating an elegant[1] settlement that leaves your children in a good place. Winning your divorce case means preserving the relationship your children have with both parents, claiming your fair share of the community property, and not wasting money on attorney fees and court costs.

Some people angrily want to hurt the other spouse. They think that if they litigate in a way that will make it very painful for the other spouse, they will win. There

---

1 An "elegant" settlement is carefully crafted and tailored to give the children and both parties the maximum benefit. It is far superior to any order a judge will fashion. It requires, however, significant attorney time and clients who allow their lawyers to negotiate.

are attorneys who will happily cater to this mindset. They profit off inflaming the negative emotions of clients who desire to inflict as much pain, financial drain and inconvenience as possible on the other spouse.

Don't let negative emotions power your divorce case

I'm not trying to downplay the emotional fallout from divorce. It can be devastating. Nevertheless, resolve those feelings with a trained therapist, a trusted friend, your pastor, prayer, or any other (and less expensive) option outside of divorce court. Remember, it is hardly a "win" to deplete yourself emotionally and financially by going after your spouse.

One ex-wife was so crushed when her ex-husband decided to marry his girlfriend that she went to his employer and accused him of violating company policy. The ex-husband's employer terminated his employment. As a result, the ex-wife had to pay the ex-husband child support due to his new loss of income. The lesson here — trying to damage your estranged spouse could end up hurting you.

In another case, a court would only allow the husband to see his children when being supervised by a professional monitor, due to his problems with prescription drugs and alcohol. After he completed 90 days of full-time residential treatment, psychological counseling, and thus addressed his problems, he attempted to get the supervision requirement lifted. The wife successfully argued that monitored visitation was still necessary, but was ordered to split the cost with him, which greatly strained her modest monetary resources. When you seek to hurt your spouse in a divorce case it can easily come back to bite you.

Judges often punish those with a vindictive mindset

Repetitive, petty squabbling over seemingly minor issues annoys judges. The judge will often favor the side that tries to resolve things in good faith, is reluctant to cause trouble, and only comes to court with genuine grievances.

The superior courts of California are overloaded with divorce and paternity cases. The judges are generally very experienced and can pick out quickly spouses who are unreasonable or vindictive. Judges expect spouses to be civil to each other and put the needs of their children above their own. If a court sees you as being vindictive or revenge seeking, it will not benefit you. You might actually get blamed for more problems than you truly caused.

Judges sometimes initiate "chambers conferences," private meetings inside judges' offices, with only lawyers present. Judges often frankly remark that one or both of the litigants are taking unreasonable positions. A judge who perceives one or both spouses as being unreasonable (or worse, vindictive) will often not rule in that party's favor.

Things are rarely "black or white" in divorce court

I have greatly enjoyed litigating thousands of family law cases. Yet, even at the end of trials that I'm certain I have won, the judge will give a partial "win" to the other side. Even clear victories are not absolute. In most cases both parties present good arguments, and both sides have their faults. Judges are human beings and they want to be perceived as being fair to both sides, so each side usually gets one or two of the things they ask for. Cases are rarely black and white; usually there is plenty of gray.[2]

There are litigants[3] who have an emotional need for a complete trial of all their issues. In other situations the other side is so unreasonable that trial is the only choice. If you are in this situation, try to schedule the trial as soon as possible.

Generally, however, most cases settle. Statistically, approximately 90% of all cases settle without trial. The goal, therefore, is to get to an elegantly crafted settlement

---

2   Each spouse has his and her own version of the truth. It has been said that "there are three sides to every case: his side, her side and the truth".

3   A "litigant" is a person involved in a lawsuit.

as soon as possible, while you still are intact emotionally and financially. Smart family law litigants choose to put their own children through college, rather than their attorney's children through college.

Winning your divorce case is working with your experienced attorney to prepare for life after divorce. Preserving your children's mental and emotional health is a huge win, not only for your children, but also for both parties.[4] It's also a victory to not expend ridiculous amounts of money on attorney fees. Winning your divorce case can mean getting out with your fair share of the community property and the property you brought into the marriage.

Winning is getting a trustworthy attorney and following his or her counsel, even in the hard moments. Winning is having realistic expectations and shortening the litigation process as much as possible. Winning is not being victimized by short-term emotions. Winning is protecting your children and your pocketbook.

---

4   Some parents discuss with the child(ren) the other parent's flaws and their anxiety. This is harmful and may leave permanent emotional scars on the children. Even worse, this thoughtless conduct can estrange the child from the other parent. This can hurt a child's self-esteem and even result in personality disorders.

chapter two
Educate Yourself First
Consult with a Family Law Specialist Attorney

Consult with an attorney who specializes in family law before you decide to divorce your spouse

Charles Kettering is reported to have said, "My interest is in the future because I am going to spend the rest of my life there."

If you are seriously considering dissolving your marriage, it's good to first count the cost and get a full understanding of the implications of what you are intending to do. There are two important aspects to consider. First, there is the emotional side. If you are somewhat undecided, you might benefit from seeing a licensed counselor or other advisor. You must also consider the financial side.

What will your life look like financially? Do not make a long term decision based on a short term emotional perspective.

Consulting with an attorney means making an appointment with a family law specialist in your county. Make sure that you tell the attorney right at the outset that you want a paid consultation and that you believe the consultation will take at least an hour. Make it clear to the attorney that you're not ready to file for divorce and that you are contemplating divorcing your spouse but not ready to do so yet. Let the attorney know that you simply want to get information about how a divorce would affect your situation.

It is very important that you do not accept a free consultation that many attorneys offer. Some attorneys offer a free consultation for the purpose of selling the potential client on the use of their services. This common practice often results in the attorney dutifully listening to your situation for a few minutes before they begin to sell you on using their law firm.

The consultation I am talking about is one that is paying for the attorney's time and expertise to fully evaluate your situation and render an opinion after listening to you carefully about how much time you can expect to have with your children in comparison with your spouse. You will also want to learn about how much support, both child support and spousal support, you could expect to receive, and how any properties you have would likely be divided. This type of consultation takes at least an hour. It is focused on educating you about how your life situation might be affected by a divorce. This consultation is not the time for a sales pitch.

You need a specialist attorney, meaning an attorney who specializes in family law. An attorney of the caliber you would want to hire will not be an attorney who gives out 60 to 90 minute free consultations. The type of attorney you want to hire to handle your marital dissolution case will be far too busy to be giving out free consultations. It will be well worth a small investment to have the right attorney carefully evaluate your case before you decide to proceed with dissolving your marriage.

When you leave this paid-for consultation you should have some notes that you have taken and a print out (one or more) of child and spousal support calculations as applicable. You may be determining the amount of support you will either pay or receive. The amount of support will depend on several factors and will be an estimate. The attorney can also create a rough balance sheet showing you how any property would likely be allocated between you and your spouse.

Second, the decision will greatly affect your finances and children. An experienced attorney who specializes in family law can offer a frank evaluation of what your life will look like should you divorce your spouse. Some of the considerations that should be evaluated include:

1. How much time will I be seeing and caring for my children if I divorce my spouse? Can I live with that?

2. If I decide to move away to a different area will that affect my ability to have custodial care of my minor children?

3. How much money can I expect to pay or receive for child and spousal support?

4. If I am not working now, at what point will the court expect me to become employed?

5. If I brought in money to the marriage from a separate source and that money was used to acquire or improve community property, to what extent can I expect to be reimbursed?

6. How will the court decide or come up with a parenting plan that is in the best interests of our children?

7. If there is domestic violence, what are my options? What if I am the perpetrator?

8. I am concerned that my spouse makes all the money and doesn't give me enough. How will I be able to pay for an attorney?

9. My spouse and I own a business which he or she manages/operates. How can I get my fair share of its value?

10. My spouse and I own a business that he manages and/or operates. He has kept me in the dark about how much money the business is making. How can I get an accurate picture of how much money my husband is making from the business?

11. What if I have signed a tax return recently prepared by my husband and the accountant that I do not believe accurately reflects our income or our deductions?

I have found that these consultations are invaluable to potential divorce litigants. Some people for whom I have done these consultations are more determined to make their existing marriages work after they've realistically contemplated their new future. Others found the consultations helped them to be realistic and gave them a plan to succeed in their future divorce litigation. These consultations usually take an hour and a half. They are very much worth doing to get a realistic assessment of what needs to be done to make your potential divorce case ready to go forward. This type of consultation will take at least an hour and possibly even two hours. However, it will pay for itself many times over and potentially serve as the basis of your case if you decide to move forward with your marital dissolution.

Dissolving your marriage is a major decision – certainly one of the most important decisions you ever make for you and for your children. Make this decision carefully after consulting all of the resources available to you.

chapter three

Hire the Right Attorney and Legal Team

If you hire the wrong plumber, you might need to redo a repair. But if you hire the wrong family law attorney, you might irreversibly harm your relationship with your children or end up completely broke. It is not an overstatement to say that choosing the right family law attorney is the most crucial decision you will make after deciding to end your marriage.

In this chapter, we will discuss how to choose the right attorney for you.

1. Hire an attorney who has a good reputation.

2. Hire a person of integrity.

3. Hire a true family law expert.

4. Hire an attorney with a winning legal team to support his or her work.

#1 Reputation

Hiring an attorney with the right reputation is paramount. As was discussed earlier, you need an attorney who has a reputation with the judge and opposing counsel as an ethical advocate for their client's best interests, not an attorney who is seen as a "jerk" or a "shark" by their colleagues.

#2 Integrity

Hire an attorney with integrity who has a legal team you have faith in. Confidence and trust are everything in this decision. If you can't trust what your attorney says and the advice he or she gives, you are wasting your resources. Above all else, you must be able to trust your attorney's integrity and expertise.

#3 Expertise

Some lawyers don't specialize in family law. They handle many types of legal issues — DUI's, criminal cases, divorces and other assorted matters. Similarly, you might have a cousin or a friend of a friend who is an attorney who doesn't specialize in divorce, but says he can handle yours. Hiring an attorney like this can be a big mistake.

When I started practicing law 25 years ago, "family law" wasn't seen by many as a complex and specialized area of law. There was the sense that any attorney could handle a divorce. If this was ever true, it is not true any longer. At a minimum, therefore, your attorney should be certified by the California State Bar as a family law specialist.

Family law is an extremely complex, fast changing, and highly specialized area of law. It requires a great deal of attention and specific training. To be a successful family law attorney, one must have considerable breadth of knowledge. This requires working knowledge that includes, but is not limited to, the following areas:

- Paternity
- Domestic violence
- Child custody
- Child Support
- Spousal support (alimony)
- Tax law
- Psychology (including personality disorders)
- Real property division
- Real estate loans and liens

- Bankruptcy law
- Pension and retirement accounts including valuation
- The time value of money and cash flow analysis
- Business valuation
- Business management
- Corporate law
- Partnership law
- Law and motion
- Discovery
- Trial work

Compared to other specialties new lawyers might choose, family law is very diverse. Your attorney must have (or be able to quickly acquire) a working knowledge of all of the above areas, to the point that your attorney can evaluate, hire and work with an expert witness for your side (or cross examine a witness from the opposing side).

Additionally, your attorney must also be an effective and persuasive writer, and be a dynamic speaker with considerable presence. They must have the physical and emotional stamina to engage in grueling trial work day after day.

#4 A winning legal team

Hire an attorney with a winning team standing behind him or her.

Even if an attorney is a person of integrity with ample expertise in family law, he or she still may lack what it takes to get winning results. It's been said that "no man is an island" — regardless of how true that is, you don't want your divorce lawyer to be one.

Some litigants think that hiring an attorney who works on his or her own without much support staff is a good idea. My experience as an attorney tells me differently. The reality is that firms that excel in family law take a team approach. The work needed to properly litigate a family law case is significant, and not all of it is attorney work. A well-supervised paralegal or legal assistant can do half of the work needed for your case.

If a very small firm is hired (an attorney working solo or with one full-time paralegal or legal assistant), the lawyer will be doing work that could be done by an assistant with a lower hourly rate. You do not want your attorney focusing on comparatively routine matters (such as preparing and propounding routine discovery requests, or gathering and organizing documents). It is expensive and it doesn't work as well.

It is also advisable to hire a lawyer who has another lawyer on staff. This "support" attorney is a talented and effective lawyer in his or her own right, who is in the office most of the time. You can call him or her any time of day and get a rapid response. The support attorney also drafts targeted discovery requests, does legal research, and drafts complicated briefs and memoranda for the lead attorney to review before they are filed. When necessary, the support attorney attends or participates in trial and is the "second chair trial attorney." They are invaluable to both you and the lead attorney for the efficient handling of your case.

chapter four

Eight Deadly Mistakes
You Can Make When
Hiring a Divorce Attorney

Mistake #1 – Hiring a "mean" attorney

You won't figure out how to get the best outcome in your divorce settlement by taking your cues from movies and TV. Nearly every popular portrayal of divorce shows one side winning by hiring a ruthless and cutthroat divorce attorney. Such a storyline may make for good drama, but it does a bad job of showing what happens in the real world.

People who make the mistake of hiring the "shark" lawyer mostly end up with empty hands and emptier pocketbooks. There are attorneys who portray themselves as the "meanest" or "nastiest" attorney in town. I've even seen one attorney who had a picture of a great white shark on his website and print advertisement.[5] Contrary to popular belief, this is usually the wrong attorney to hire. Attorneys who act or market themselves as deliberately nasty can also be extremely egotistical and difficult to work with.

Attorneys of this type prey on the unsuspecting clients who want to use the process not to fairly adjudicate the case, but instead to bludgeon the other spouse. If you are looking for this type of attorney please do not contact my office. These attorneys get a good number of new clients who think they now have an attorney who can "beat up" their spouse. And these attorneys often laugh all the way to the bank with their huge retainer checks paid by the unsuspecting client.

I have dealt with these attorneys for 25 years. Thankfully they are a relative minority of working attorneys. Many of their clients hire me after firing them. Remember, the same cutthroat quality you want to weaponize against your spouse will eventually destroy your own attorney-client relationship and you will likely be on the receiving end of the ruthlessness you hired.

This is not the kind of attorney who will settle your case expeditiously, leaving you money in your estate. Instead, this type of attorney may "churn" (over litigate)

---

5   Not every attorney, however, who uses this sort of imagery, is the type of bad attorney we are discussing. He or she may be a good attorney who is merely trying to attract new clients. That said, this sort of marketing imagery is a red flag, and you should bypass working with any attorney who says that this is his or her *modus operandi.*

your case until your funds are gone. Then the case will likely be settled, because there's nothing else to be gained by the lawyer. This attorney is often lazy, and really has little interest in doing anything but systematically transferring your money from your bank account into his or hers.

Mistake #2 – Hiring a "door attorney"

This attorney accepts any case that comes through the door. He advertises as an attorney who can do all types of work. Run from this attorney. In this age of specialization, an attorney who does not have a specialty is a disaster waiting to happen. He cannot compete with attorneys who have specialized training. He is simply desperate for work. You do not want an attorney to be learning the basics of family law on your dime while he is getting "schooled" by your spouse's attorney.

Mistake #3 – Hiring a "bargain attorney"

Some attorneys claim to be willing to work for a fraction of what other attorneys charge. In almost all cases, hiring this kind of attorney is a bad idea. We live in a society where professionals demand to be paid according to their worth. The bargain attorney usually is not equipped to deal with anything but the very simplest case. The bargain attorney usually does not have a legal team or the capability to handle a case of any significant magnitude. The old adage, "You get what you pay for," could not be more true when hiring a family law attorney.

Mistake #4 – Failing to carefully interview the attorney

It is important to interview a potential attorney before you agree to sign up with him or her. You can learn a lot in an interview. Do you have to wait very long for your appointment to begin? Look at the office of the attorney you are interviewing, as it is usually a reflection of that attorney. Is the office cluttered and disorganized? Observe his or her staff. Do they appear to be calm and happy to work there? When you tell the attorney about your case, do you get her full attention, or is she preoccupied with other matters? Does he make you feel uneasy? Is this a person you would like to work with? Ask your prospective attorney why you should hire him or her. Ask about his staff, including which of them will be working on your case. Take the opportunity to meet them. Do they make you feel comfortable and confident? If your gut feeling gives you concern, listen to it and go elsewhere.

Mistake #5 – Hiring a lawyer who does not listen to you

When you interview a prospective attorney make sure that person is giving you his or her full attention. This person will rarely be more focused on you and your unique situation than in your initial interview, when he or she is trying to sell you on the firm. Ask your attorney open-ended questions to ascertain whether or not he or she understands what you're saying. Listening is the key to communication. You must be able to communicate with your lawyer.

Mistake #6 – Hiring a lawyer who does not specialize in family law

Family law is a very specialized field. A lawyer who tries to dabble in family law can easily be left bleeding by a specialist in the field. I recommend that a prospective attorney only be hired to head up your case if he or she is a specialist in family law who is board certified by the State Bar of California. Successful attorneys are specialized and do not "dabble" in other fields of law.

Mistake #7 – Deciding not to hire a lawyer or signing an agreement with your spouse without consulting a competent attorney

Self-representation is almost always a bad idea. Without professional help and advice, you are playing roulette with your money and family. It doesn't matter if you think your spouse has not hired an attorney. Mediation of your case without an attorney has the potential for disaster.

There is one circumstance where it's probably OK to "do it yourself" with your spouse — if you both decide to forego hiring an attorney, you have been married a year or less and you have no children or assets to divide. If this is the case, the two of you can probably work it out without counsel. Otherwise, get a lawyer. You are dealing with your kids, your money, and your future. You need a competent and trusted legal advisor who has your back. Therefore, avoid signing any agreement without consulting a competent attorney.[6]

A mediator will not suffice. A mediator is not your attorney, so he or she won't put your interests first. A mediator's job is to get a settlement. I have seen clients literally lose hundreds of thousands of dollars because they decided to go to a mediator and not hire an attorney. Hiring an attorney is not synonymous with wanting to

---

6   You might be able to have a signed agreement set aside if only a few months have passed, but you will likely be ordered to pay some or all of the other side's attorney fees in addition to your own attorney fees. Better to pay an attorney at the outset.

fight. Rather, having an experienced lawyer is prudent to protect your future. Any good mediator will not discourage you from having counsel, but instead will encourage you to fully involve an attorney in the mediation process.

Gullible and unwise spouses choose to work with a mediator and without counsel. Often one spouse lures the other spouse into the mediation without counsel, while an attorney in the background is carefully advising him or her. So one spouse has legal advice, and the other spouse naïvely participates without one. Guess which spouse wins in this common situation?

Never participate in any meaningful mediation or settlement meeting without an attorney by your side. Absolutely never sign any agreement without first consulting a competent attorney who specializes in family law. Any legitimate mediator will want you to have counsel.

Mistake #8 - Failing to replace an attorney who has lost your confidence

Sometimes, no matter how hard you (and perhaps your attorney) try, you may find that the attorney-client relationship is not working. Listen to your gut. If something does not seem right, question your attorney about it and make sure you get an answer. If your bill seems unfair, raise your concerns in writing immediately. Many attorneys have a clause in their client fee agreements that requires the client to object in writing to any charge on their bill they feel is excessive or improper within a few days of receiving the invoice.

If you are not feeling good about your attorney's services, tell him or her about your concerns. If you have hired a good attorney, he or she and the staff will bend over backwards to make things right. If they do so and things get better, this is evidence that you have hired an attorney and legal team who are responsive to your needs. If you are not satisfied with the legal care you have been getting, start with step one above and seek out a second opinion from another attorney who specializes in family law.

Remember that this is your life. As someone once said: "Life is not a dress rehearsal." It's crucial that you maintain a relationship of trust and confidence in your attorney. If your attorney deliberately lies to you or misleads you, run. The process of dissolving your marriage is stressful enough as it is. You must have an attorney and legal team in your corner that you fully trust.

chapter five

File for Divorce *BEFORE* Your Spouse Does

Once you have resolved to end your marriage, it is very important that you file the initial petition first. You don't have to serve the paperwork right away, but be the first to file.

The main reason to file your divorce case first is that the first person to file the case becomes the petitioner, and at the trial the petitioner presents his or her case first. In any situation, being able to present your case first is a substantial advantage. But it is an even greater advantage in a California superior court.

It is very important to be the petitioner. You should file the papers first. If the matter goes to trial, the petitioner puts his or her case on first. This is a great advantage. Also, the last person to file, the respondent, must quickly retain legal counsel and protect their rights to stay in the family home and see the children — without the benefit of preparation and foresight.

Once the summons and petition are filed, the parties are considered at least partially separated. It is still most common that the wife is the first spouse to file for divorce. In general, the wife is also still typically the primary caretaker of the children and the husband the primary breadwinner. (Of course, this is not always the case.) If the spouses are living separately, the wife is often seeking financial support and the husband is seeking time with the children.

Sometimes the separation is precipitated by a violent event where one or both spouses physically attack the other. Sometimes police are called. In most of these cases the judge will set up a formal visitation schedule called a parenting plan, and the household income will now need to be allocated between the parties, who will most likely be living separately. These financial and visitation "orders" are encompassed in a document called "temporary orders," and it helps the parties move forward with as little conflict as possible.

When the case gets to trial, you'll likely have to end early because of the court's limited docket. The party who is able to present their opening statement and testimony of witnesses and exhibits gains an advantage. Your spouse and his or her attorney will have to wait until your case is finished before they can put on their case.

There are therefore numerous advantages for being able to present your case first. First impressions are hard to overcome. You may have heard the saying "you never get a second chance to make a good first impression." Judges are human beings. If your attorney presents your case first and persuasively, your spouse and his or her attorney will have a huge uphill battle to climb when they finally are allowed to present their case. Judges are affected (and even somewhat prejudiced) against the respondent and his or her case if they like the case the petitioner has already put on. It is just human nature to be drawn in by an effective presentation of compelling witnesses, testimony and exhibits.

Judges have a lot of work to do, with many cases to handle. They're task oriented and want to get a handle on each case as soon as possible. In an ideal world, a judge would listen to the petitioner's case, and reserve judgment until they had given the respondent equal time. In the real world, however, it's hard for them to remain completely unmoved by an effectively presented case. I have seen judges become impatient with the presentation of the respondent's case when the judge thinks they already know the facts.

One day several years ago I was putting on a complete and compelling presentation of my client's case. Fortunately, my client was the petitioner. My opening statement detailed how the evidence showed that the respondent's substance abuse put his children in danger.

The court had only heard my opening statement and my client's testimony and cross-examination. Surprisingly, the judge called a recess and called the attorneys back into his judicial chambers. The judge sat back in his high backed chair and said to the other attorney, "what do you have that will refute all this?" The other attorney was visibly taken aback, and sputtered that he had not presented his case yet. He implied that he had plenty of evidence in his client's favor. The judge was not having any of it. He reiterated his question and demanded to know what evidence their side had to refute my client's testimony. The judge then indicated he wanted both sides to go outside the courtroom and try to settle. Being able to present my case first was therefore a huge advantage.

Furthermore, as discussed previously, trials that have started are often delayed. If this occurs and your partially completed trial must be put off for weeks or months, it is an advantage to have your case presented first and that presentation as the last thing on the judge's mind.

There is no question that filing your divorce case first and thus being the first to present your case at trial is very beneficial. Even if you're not sure which attorney you want to hire, you can pay an attorney's office to simply file the paperwork in your name. You can subsequently hire an attorney who will then take over the case. Just be sure to file your case first.

Be aware, however, that once you file for divorce, it becomes public record and your spouse may find out quickly. There are entities that collect all new dissolution filings and they might send a letter to your spouse alerting him or her. This can obviously cause drama and problems. Even if someone is aware that his or her marriage is on the rocks, learning by mail of the divorce case can be a shock. Keep this in mind when you file.

chapter six

Your Family Court Judge

Understanding the judge selection process and the mindset of a typical judge will help you choose the right attorney to present yourself and your case.

Getting the right judge is crucial – he or she will stay with your case to the end

Your case will be assigned randomly to a family law judge who handles exclusively family law matters. While your attorney may be able to initially navigate away from one or more judges in the very beginning, once your case is assigned to a particular judge you will usually be stuck with that judge. This has several important implications.

To get the right judge, hire a local attorney who knows the local family court judges

An attorney who is familiar with your county's judges would know if the judge you are tentatively assigned to would be sympathetic to your case. For example, I practice primarily in Orange County. I'm very familiar with these judges and their local rules.

Every judge has his or her own life experiences and sensitivities. Some are divorced themselves. Some are liberal and some are conservative. Some are more inclined to favor mothers over fathers in custody disputes, and vice versa. An inexperienced attorney will not be helpful in this initial important stage of "judge shopping."

Self-representation is a bad idea and annoys judges

Judges are lawyers themselves and prefer to deal with lawyers. Self-represented parties frustrate them. Law, like other professions such as medicine or engineering, involves a complex language and set of rules that non-lawyers can only partially understand.

Judges have the very difficult job of having to resolve a huge number of cases each year. Judges know that experienced lawyers can usually move the case along faster and take less of the court's[7] time. Judges depend on lawyers to resolve as much of the case as possible. Without the lawyers doing this, the already crowded court system could not function. Hiring an experienced family law

---

7   The terms "judge" and "court" are interchangeable and refer to the judicial officer presiding over your case.

specialist attorney who knows your county's judges is therefore critical.

Attorneys with good reputations are more respected by judges

An attorney with a good reputation is known to be ethical, honest, and assertive without being a "shark" or a jerk. Judges prefer experienced, honest and genuine lawyers. Your judge likely knows your lawyer — either from previous court hearings or as a colleague when the judge practiced law. If you choose a "shark," "killer" or unethical attorney, the judge will therefore likely also be aware of your attorney's reputation. This type of reputation might appeal to someone who is emotionally devastated by the divorce. But the lawyer with that type of reputation will often be resented and disliked just as much by the judge as by other attorneys.

Cutthroat attorneys who are hated by their colleagues might prevail in Hollywood movies, but it's a terrible idea in real life. Your attorney's good reputation may result in the judge giving you the benefit of the doubt. The converse is also true — an attorney's bad reputation could tarnish your credibility.

Some lawyers have a reputation for taking every case to trial — to the client's great expense. Judges have crowded court dockets and tend to dislike attorneys who insist on trying every case. Unfortunately, the judge may hold this prejudice against the client. Remember — judges are former attorneys who now serve the public. They have limited time and patience for attorneys and parties deemed unreasonable.

Make the right first impression on the judge

The old saying "you never get a second chance to make a first impression" applies aptly to judges. First impressions don't easily change and judges could make important decisions based on them.

Ethical attorneys with good reputations put judges at ease. They know your attorney will protect you and handle your case properly. Even judges who try to stay impartial will not relish dealing with an attorney with a bad reputation. And, unfortunately, that will most likely result in a less than optimal outcome for you.

My county has attorneys with well-earned reputations as being nasty or unpleasant. Some are very unethical and will make litigation unpleasant and cost consuming. Judges must monitor these attorneys closely, as they will deliberately and dishonestly misrepresent and overstate their cases and attempt one dirty trick after another.

One day I was sitting with my client in the court gallery[8] waiting for our case to be called. One such attorney with a bad reputation was making a ludicrous and overstated argument. The other attorney said, "Mrs. Smith [not her real name] is misstating the facts [in case she refers to]. That case stands for exactly the opposite point." The judge then rolled his eyes in agreement and stated, "Counsel, I know Mrs. Smith. I knew her and practiced against her when I was an attorney. I will give her argument the weight that it deserves." This unethical attorney's past conduct prejudiced the court[9] against the client's case.

Do this: Hire an experienced family law specialist who works regularly in your county. Make sure your lawyer and his or her firm has a good reputation. You are looking for someone who can be an effective and zealous advocate for your interests without alienating the judge or colleagues. Trust them to navigate away from judges who would not be good for your case.

Don't do this: Don't hire a lawyer who has the reputation of being "mean," a "shark," or unethical. You will regret it when you get your day in court, and especially if you eventually owe him or her money.

---

8   The gallery is the courtroom area where the public is allowed to sit, behind the attorneys' tables and the short wall called the "bar."

9   The term "court" as used here refers to the judge, not the system or courtroom.

chapter seven

Protect Yourself Online

Protect yourself electronically

You can be sharing photographs and other information on social media that you believe is harmless. Yet that information can be absolutely deadly to your ability to get custody of your children. In this age of pervasive technology there are many ways your spouse can have access to information you thought was private.[10]

Change all passwords

Assume at this time that your spouse knows all of your passwords to your email accounts, even if you never specifically gave him or her that information. He or she

---

10 Far too many times I have seen spouses have access to the other spouse's emails or texts. This is especially true when the other spouse has been in charge of the family cell phone account.

likely also has the passcode to get into your cell phone. Some spouses can be extremely possessive and snoopy. Your electronic communications such as emails and texts are intended to be private. However, very likely, they are not as secure as you believe, especially in a long-term marriage. You may also have even given your spouse your passwords to various things over time. Your spouse is likely to know what your preferred passwords are or to know what things you tend to base your passwords on. With some trial and error, your spouse can likely determine your current passwords. Choose new, secure passwords that are different from previous passwords. Pick ones that are unlikely to be guessed by your spouse.

Get a new email address

Prior to your divorce or paternity action, get a new email address and do not give it out. Use this more private email address to communicate with your attorney. Communicate with your estranged spouse on your former email address. You simply cannot afford for your spouse to have access to your emails. I can assure you this happens, and not infrequently.

One of my clients told me that she believed her husband had the ability to get into and read her email and text messages. This distressed client believed her husband had installed a program on her laptop and desktop computer that could monitor her keystrokes. I felt extremely uncomfortable communicating with her in any manner except by cell phone.

Change your passwords to everything — your email, computer, laptop, messaging apps, cell phone, etc. Get whatever technical advice and help you need to make sure that your electronic communications are secure.

Finally, make sure that you clear out the history on your computer if you have been researching anything pertaining to a divorce. And know that your household network is not secure from subsequent research by your spouse. Meaningful searches will best be done off of your phone or on your computer at work.

Clean up or close your social media accounts

If you do not close your social media accounts, be very careful what photographs are on them, and anything you say or have said on them. Pictures on social media that show you partying or with a drink in your hand do not play well in court when you are trying to present the image of a good parent wanting custody of your children.

In addition, complaining about your spouse, your case, or anything that may have happened in court on social media is a huge mistake. Never complain about the judge assigned to your case or rulings that he or she made on social media. When you are in a divorce, anything you ever have posted on your Facebook, Instagram, or other social media accounts can easily be used against you.

Not long ago I was hired by a woman with a teenage son with some special needs. She'd previously had some difficulty with the judge assigned to her case and felt that he had treated her unfairly. She posted complaints about the judge on a website which rated judges. We lost a subsequent hearing that it seemed we should have won. This judge was obviously aware of what my client had said about him.

Do not, therefore, bad mouth your judge or others important to your case on the internet. No matter how upset you are, never make public comments about it; you should even be careful about which friends you choose to disclose your situation to.

In general, when you are in the midst of a divorce case, be very careful about what you say and do, and whom you are in front of, especially when people are taking pictures.

Some time ago I had a client who had recently been convicted for DUI. He was fighting to have time with his three young children to whom he was a loving and caring father. The court ordered him to not use alcohol when his children were in his care. He got remarried while he was still fighting for his children. At his wedding several photos were taken of him drinking champagne. These were reported back to his wife, who brought it in front of the court. This unfortunate situation resulted in decreased time with his children.

Two lessons can be learned from that unfortunate incident. First, never disobey court orders. Second, even your purported friends could report you when you are doing something wrong, especially when it involves children.

Are you being electronically tracked?

In a divorce situation, your spouse will likely be curious whom you are talking to and where you're going. It is not unusual for estranged spouses to have you followed, or even install a GPS device on your vehicle. This permits your spouse to track and know where your vehicle is at all times. I have had clients who found proof that their abusive and controlling spouse was doing this to them. You may also be unknowingly sharing your location with your spouse via your mobile phone. Get whatever technical help you need to make sure that phone is secured from your spouse and you are not "sharing your location" via your phone's inbuilt geotracking device/geolocator. Resetting your phone to its factory settings and setting a new passcode is a good start.

One of my clients told me that she had left her children with her husband to privately to talk a friend on her cell phone. She drove approximately five miles away to a place she believed she could never be found — the empty parking lot of a church she was not a member of. Imagine her surprise when her husband drove up 20 minutes later.

There are very obvious reasons why you would not want your spouse you know where you are, and particularly whether you are at home or not. If your spouse has any significant history of being abusive or controlling, assume that he or she is trying to track your movements and govern yourself accordingly. Do what you need to do to stay safe.

In conclusion, plan to get the documents you need as early as possible. Assume that your spouse has also talked to an attorney and is making similar plans to protect him or herself. Take any and all steps available to make sure that your electronic communications are protected and confidential.

chapter eight

Win by Mental Preparation

Meet with a therapist

There are many reasons to have a good therapist. If you and your spouse are in marriage counseling, it wouldn't hurt to ask your marriage counselor privately if he or she believes your marriage can be saved or whether it would be better for you to take the next step of dissolving your marriage. Listen carefully to what your therapist tells you, and be willing to accept that you may be part of the problem. If you believe in your heart that your marriage can be saved, consider continuing to work on your marriage and forgiving your spouse. On the other hand, if you feel differently after talking your therapist, it may be time to proceed.

If you decide to proceed with the divorce, you might experience an emotional upheaval. Many of my clients go through profound stages of depression and grief. I am willing to listen because I care about what they are feeling. However, a therapist, or even a trusted friend, is a much less expensive sounding board than an attorney, and a therapist can give the client much better advice and grieving tools than I can.

I have, on rare occasions, referred my clients who had already filed divorce papers to a marriage counselor. One particular marriage counselor I have sent clients to has resulted in a number of clients putting their divorce cases on hold. Many marriages can be saved if the parties will both "put down their swords" and be willing to look inwardly on how they could be a better spouse to the person they once promised to love and support "till death do us part." Patience, forgiving your spouse, and seeking forgiveness from your spouse is an essential part of any successful and lasting marriage.

All of us must realize that we are imperfect people, and that each of us has some level of dysfunction and possibly even mental illness. If our mental illness affects us to the point that we cannot function appropriately in our family life, we may need to seek out a mental health professional. Sometimes, in addition to regular therapy with a psychologist, some litigants may need to be on medication (even temporarily) to deal with depression and other conditions. I have seen situations where the court orders parties to be psychiatrically evaluated. It's better to address this on your own, rather than having a judge order you to do it.

Where there is addiction and/or frequent use of alcohol, prescription or nonprescription drugs, a party may be forced by a court to be evaluated by a substance abuse expert. If you are in this situation, have an attorney protect your rights under California Family Code Section 4150.[11] In any event, if you are found to be an abuser of substances, you will likely be forced to get help such as regularly going to Alcoholics Anonymous or Narcotics Anonymous. You will also likely be required to undergo therapy sessions with a mental health professional.

High conflict divorces – personality disorders

Sometimes there are psychological factors that make divorce even harder. If one (or both) spouses suffer from mental illness, there is the potential for even more serious and protracted problems that affect the marital relationship, the divorce process, and the children. Some spouses may have a personality disorder, such as:

1. Borderline personality disorder

---

11   California Family Code Section 4150 limits the court's ability to require substance or alcohol abuse testing to situations where there is evidence the party has abused these substances, as opposed to merely having used them.

2. Histrionic personality disorder

3. Narcissistic personality disorder

4. Bipolar disorder

People with the above conditions can make a marriage or family life extremely difficult and even heartbreaking. They are "frequent fliers" in divorce cases. These people often present themselves as extremely intelligent, charismatic, warm and fun. They are often very talented and accomplished people. But there is significant contention and craziness that is often only observed by his or her immediate family.

If you are divorcing a person with any of the above conditions (whether officially diagnosed or not), you need an attorney who understands how to deal with these kinds of people. I recommend that clients in these situations read a book written by family law attorney, mediator, and therapist, William Eddy, entitled, *Splitting: Protecting Yourself while Divorcing Someone with Borderline or Narcissistic Personality Disorder.* If you are divorcing somebody with these traits, you had better hold on for what will be a very difficult ride. This book will help you understand what is going on with you and your spouse. It will be a guide on how to deal with the divorce and protect your children to the fullest extent possible. Bill Eddy has written several books on the subject of high conflict divorces.

In my experience, this type of high conflict litigant has a difficult time settling the case. They have delusions of grandeur and often relish the thought of a final confrontation at trial. They are not to be underestimated as opponents, and sometimes the borderline or high conflict client will also have a borderline or high conflict attorney. This makes things extra difficult. You must have an attorney who understands these types of litigants. The process of getting them to trial must be expedited.

Typically a high conflict spouse will send many disturbing text, email, and phone messages that will make you crazy if you get caught up in them. In his book, Bill Eddy recommends that you limit communications with your spouse and that they follow what is known as BIFF. BIFF stands for:

B – Brief

I – Informative

F – Friendly

F – Firm

Sometimes communication between high conflict spouses may be such a problem that it needs to be documented. Two different email programs were created to help parents communicate information about their children with each other: "Our Family Wizard" and "Talking Parents."

Both of these programs are designed to facilitate easy and conflict-free communication between parents about information related to their children. Attorneys and judges can later read these communications.

In conclusion, if you think you're headed for divorce, consult with an expert attorney, at least one therapist, and any therapists involved with you and your spouse. Get their frank assessments. Talk to your parents and very close friends. Then, make the best decision you can. If you are divorcing a spouse with a personality disorder or mental illness, hire an attorney experienced with high-conflict cases and keep your communications with your spouse brief, informative, friendly, and firm.

chapter nine

Win by Physical Preparation

Prepare your documents

It is extremely important to gather as many documents as you can as soon as possible. Your spouse may consider the business that was started and built up during the marriage to be his or hers rather than a business belonging to both of you. Even if your spouse's business started operating prior to your marriage, the same rules apply; a portion of the increase in value that occurred during the marriage is often considered community property. Therefore, get your hands on as many documents as possible before your spouse thinks you might be divorcing him or her.

There are other reasons for getting documents early. You can't fairly adjudicate your divorce until you have needed information. Once your spouse knows that you may be seeking a divorce, he or she may make it more difficult for you to get these documents. And that is one way that divorces really get stalled. It can take months and a great deal of money to get documents that you could have gathered on your own.

Another important reason to get documents early is that there are authentication problems with documents that are more than seven years old. For a document to be admissible as evidence in a court of law, the document must be proven to be authentic. To get an authenticated document, it usually needs to come directly to the court from the entity (such as the bank) that generated the document. Unfortunately, most financial institutions only keep copies of records for seven years. Older documents, however, can be authenticated in a deposition.[12] In order to make that happen, the deposition should be taken early in the process. The longer you wait, the more your spouse will become aware of the importance of certain documents, and his or her right to refuse to authenticate them.

Once you have any needed documents, it is important to prepare a safe place to keep them. I have had a number of clients whose spouse was able to find their stash of documents. Divorce is war. Assume your spouse will stop at nothing to protect him or herself. Keep your important

---

12 A deposition is the examination of a person by an attorney with a court reporter. The person being deposed answers questions under penalty of perjury. A transcript of the questions and answers, including any exhibits and documents, are then put into a transcript for use at any future legal proceeding. It is essentially an opportunity to find out what a person's testimony will be before a formal hearing takes place.

documents in a safe place that is not in your home or vehicle — such as a safe in your parent's home or the home of a trusted friend.

Safeguard divorce documents if you continue to live together

Many people continue living under the same roof, sometimes for a long time, after a divorce is initiated. You will receive many important documents and communications from your attorney and others after you file for divorce. These documents need to be kept safe from your spouse. Find a safe place to keep them where your spouse cannot get to them. Assume if you are living in the same residence, even if in separate rooms, that your spouse will enter your private room and get into any "safe" place you think you have created.

If you decide to continue cohabitating, consider renting a post office mailbox and instruct your attorney to send your documents and bills to this secure mailing address. The monthly statement your attorney sends you will often have confidential information in the description of the work you are being charged for.

chapter ten
Financial Preparation

Getting a divorce can be expensive. The high cost of divorce is one reason for the writing of this book. When the high cost of an attorney and his or her legal team is coupled with the inefficiency of the court process, the result is a perfect storm. Hence, the need to get your case out of the public court system to a private judge or mediator as soon as possible.

Any attorney who is competent and experienced will require at least $5,000 as a retainer to get started. Your retainer is a deposit that future services will be billed against by your attorney and his or her legal team at their hourly rates. When your retainer is close to being used up, your attorney will require that you deposit additional funds to bill against. This is a reality of litigation. Your lawyer will have one or more of his staff who are responsible to make sure that monies are on deposit for he and his staff to bill against.

Need based attorney fee awards

Money is generally a concern. You want to be very careful with it. Sometimes your spouse may have much greater access to money than you do. Often there is a disparity in the respective access to funds between the parties. If your spouse has greater access to funds then you do, you can request that the court order your spouse to pay you money to level the playing field with regard to attorney fees. This is called a Family Code 2030-2033 "need-based" attorney fee award. If you are in the disadvantaged position, you need to make an attorney fee requests from the court early and often. This is an important part of your case. You must have the ability to finance your case.

Conduct-based attorney fees i.e. sanctions

Attorney fees can also be ordered (pursuant to California Family Code Section 271) for conduct on the part of the other party and/or his or her attorney that is deemed to frustrate a prompt settlement of your case. This type of award is known as a sanction. Sanctions can be awarded from one party payable to the other (or even the court) for many types of conduct that increases the cost to the other side. There are many examples of this, from the filing of a request that does not have legal substance, to failing to answer discovery requests promptly.

Get the best lawyer you can. If your spouse has greater access to cash than you do, ask the court to award you money to allow you to hire an attorney or to contribute to the fees charged by the attorney you have already hired. Make these requests early and often.

chapter eleven

Mediate Your Case Early With Both Sides Having Attorneys

Mediation is the opportunity for both sides to meet with a neutral third-party and attempt to informally resolve their dispute. The process is completely confidential and nothing that is said can be used by either party in any future proceeding.

Mediations are beneficial because they allow the parties and their attorneys to quickly discuss issues without interruption and focus on areas of disagreement. These areas can be negotiated in a spirit of cooperation. When sufficient information is available to both sides, a skilled mediator can often tailor a beneficial agreement that is more suited to your particular situation than a judge will.

I was in court one day on a case where parents were fighting over how to share their children. The judge took his seat and said to the parents, "I am offended that the two of you cannot decide what is best for your children, the people you love more than anybody, and that you would leave such a decision to me, a total stranger."

When the mediator is a skilled family law attorney or retired judge mediator, you are in good hands. These professionals have great experience in breaking stalemates. I am often amazed when I participate in the successful mediation of very difficult cases, some that I was certain wouldn't have settled.

Not only are the outcomes better, the aftermath of mediation tends to be better as well. In my experience, parties that mediate are generally much nicer with each other afterwards. People tend to be better able to work together for the sake of their children after a mediated settlement as opposed to a verdict from a judge.

Having an attorney in mediation is crucial. The mediator cannot give legal advice to either side. It hurts his or her neutrality. Each spouse needs a legal advisor who knows the situation to advise him or her in these crucial situations.

Some spouses object to paying for a third professional when a public court judge does not cost additional money. However, mediation is a bargain because the mediator can focus completely on your whole case at one time. Courts break up issues into numerous hearings. So the judge is just getting a piece of your case each time, and busy courts can delay these hearing.

Neither side will be 100 percent happy with the result of mediation. Yet, the compromise that is reached is according to the law, and more importantly, is hopefully acceptable enough to both sides so that both parties can move forward without additional litigation and its attendant costs.

I once had two close friends who were divorcing. Our families had been in the same church congregation and the husband and I typically jogged together every morning. I did not represent either of them because they were both close friends. The husband described going to mediation with their attorneys and how they both decided that each would take the children for one half of the time and that each would keep their own separate professional practice. No support would be paid from either party to the other. The house would be sold and the proceeds divided equally. Although they were right at the cusp of a mediated settlement, they ended up not settling.

Eighteen months later they had spent over $100,000 each on attorneys to go trial. The outcome was the same outcome as the mediated settlement. No less than $200,000 later, the only thing they won was increased animosity for each other.

Mediate your case early with a competent attorney by your side and never sign any documents without his or her approval.

chapter twelve

Navigating the Public Court System

If you don't take control of your case early on, your divorce will likely take at least a full year to complete if you stay in the public court system. If you have significant issues to fight over, your divorce will more likely take much longer to complete. It is not unusual for a divorce in the public court system to take at least a year and a half to two years to complete. Below is a roadmap of the typical steps or hoops a party must jump through to reach the finish of a divorce.

Major landmarks in a "typical" case roadmap:

1. Initial filing of petition and response, and judge selection

2. Temporary (pendente lite) orders hearings

3. Discovery

4. Law and motion

5. Trial setting conference

6. Mandatory settlement conference(s)

7. Trial

8. Post judgment matters

Is there a better way, you may think? The answer is yes. The typical divorce case roadmap is long, and can be expensive. Thankfully, many cases can be handled without going through all of these steps. In fact, most parties are better served by not going through all of them.

Now let's go through the eight steps that are present on the roadmap of the typical Southern California divorce case:

1. THE INITIAL FILING OF A PETITION AND RESPONSE

The spouse who files for divorce will first file a petition and a summons. Both of these documents are required to be personally served on the other spouse. Any adult (except the filing spouse) can do this. Usually, however, a professional process server does it.

Once your spouse has been "served" the summons and petition (and other ancillary documents), the responding spouse must file a response within 30 days. The spouse who filed a petition is called the "petitioner." The spouse who filed the response is called the "respondent."

In certain cases, and especially where there is domestic violence, these temporary orders are made quickly — sometimes within days.[13] More frequently, it takes a few weeks to sort out the facts and allocate the children (and the money) between the parties.

Selection of a judge

A case is assigned to a judge and given a hearing date after a party files a "request for orders," which is necessary to obtain temporary orders. The 10-day clock to object to the assigned judge starts when the party receives the request. Each attorney may object to the judicial assignment one time. If either attorney files an objection, a different judicial officer is assigned.

---

13   When domestic violence occurs, often police will remove the allegedly violent spouse from the family home, or he or she will leave voluntarily. Within two days a temporary restraining order (called a TRO) could be issued, which keeps the accused spouse out of the home for up to 21 days. Within 21 days the party temporarily removed from the residence is entitled to a hearing. At the hearing, if the court decides that no violence occurred, he or she may be allowed to move back into the family home. If the court, however, finds that domestic violence occurred and one party was the primary aggressor, that party will not be allowed to move back in and could also have an uphill battle in custody issues. Temporary child custody and monetary orders can also be made at domestic violence hearings.

The decision whether to object is a judgment call which should be made by your attorney, and there's no guarantee that the new judge will be any more preferable. It's a complicated decision with many variables and moving parts. Your best move is to hire a competent, skilled, and experienced attorney, and then to step back and let the attorney make his or her judgment call on the best action to take. Once both sides have had the opportunity to object, the judicial officer assigned to the case will remain on the case and is more or less your permanent judge, with rare exceptions.

2. HEARINGS FOR TEMPORARY ORDERS

If the parties can't agree on the children's visitation and living arrangements, and/or how earnings will be allocated to both sides, each party will have the opportunity to go to court for a hearing on temporary (pending litigation) orders.14

The written request for temporary orders forms discussed above usually contains substantial written declarations from both parties. These sworn declarations state each party's side of the story and why they should be given a certain amount of time with the children, as

---

14 Temporary or "pendente lite" orders are orders made without a trial, pending a future trial or other hearing. They decide the temporary custody, parenting plans (visitation), and child/spousal support. The judge will base his or her decision on written declarations of the parties and oral argument.

well as other relief (including, but not limited to, certain restraining orders).

As discussed above, domestic violence restraining order hearings are held as early as 21 days into the case. These hearings are usually the fastest way to get temporary custody and support orders. The temporary order hearings usually center on how much access each spouse will have to the children, pending the trial or the end of the case. Temporary child and spousal support awards are also made at these hearings. These temporary custody and support orders can be changed by the court (or by the parties) if they agree before trial, and if circumstances dictate.

a. Custody orders

Children are the most important part of any family law case or dispute. Their emotional and physical comfort and well-being is paramount to all other issues the parties may fight over.

b. Mandatory mediation

If temporary orders regarding the custody of the children are sought by one or both parties, the court will set a temporary order hearing date and the parties will be ordered to attend mandatory custody mediation. The mandatory custody mediation will occur at least a few days before the scheduled hearing for temporary orders. Child custody mediation is typically mandatory before a judge will make an order regarding custody of your children. The mediation requires preparation. Your attorney will not be with you in the mediation but you should seek out his or her advice beforehand.

At the mandatory mediation, you will listen to a presentation encouraging the spouses to agree on a parenting plan that best serves your children. Afterwards, you will have the opportunity to sit down with your spouse and an impartial professional mediator to attempt to work out a parenting plan. Only after you have completed this process will a court be willing to decide how you and your spouse will share your children.15

c. Hearing

The next step in the process is the actual hearing for the temporary orders on custody, support, and other financial or restraining orders. These hearings are usually held in the morning. You will find yourself going to court and being there no later than 8:30 AM. This can be

---

15   In San Diego, Riverside, and San Bernardino counties, the mediation process differs. Trained mediators actually interview the parties and sometimes the children. Then the mediator (also known as a family court services worker) makes a written recommendation to the judge of a parenting plan deemed to be in the children's best interests. These recommendations are often followed by the court pending trial or future hearings.

a nerve-racking experience. It is likely the first time you will meet the judge who will decide your case. It may also be the first time you meet the attorney who represents your spouse. Plan to be at court all morning (and possibly all day) so that you can eventually get 15 to 20 minutes of the court's time.

Neither you nor your spouse will likely testify at the request for order hearing. There simply is not time. The court likely has up to 10 other similar matters to attend to that morning. Your attorney is expected to negotiate with the other side to see if an agreement can be made regarding custody, child/spousal support, and on any other matters that are requested in the request for order. The court usually does not have time to do much beyond making orders that are based on the written declarations he or she has (hopefully) read. It is possible to have a hearing that can last up to an hour or two, but in my experience it is highly unlikely. Notwithstanding all of the above, your attorney must be prepared, in the rare event that the court actually has time to hear witness testimony on your case.

After your hearing, you will leave court with a temporary parenting plan and temporary support orders. You may also leave court with an impression that notwithstanding the work you and your attorney put in creating your temporary orders request, the judge did not fully read it.[16] Certainly, you will feel disappointed if you expected the judge to be familiar with the fine points of your case. It will seem like you spent a lot of money preparing for a mini-trial that did not really happen. You will likely sense that more work needs to be done in your case to achieve your desired result. And you will have a much greater understanding of how inefficient the California family law court system can be.

The overworked judges are not to be blamed for the problem of overcrowded family courts. They are simply participants in the system that is too crowded. Superior court judges are usually responsible for at least two thousand other family law cases. On the day you go to court for your temporary orders hearing, your judge will have about three hours to work through about 10 other similar requests for temporary orders. And they must get through them by noon. The court is then closed for lunch until 1:30 PM. After lunch, the court assigned to your case usually has an entirely different calendar to handle. Usually, there are one or two trials that are set for the same afternoon time period each day. Don't, therefore, blame the judge for not conducting an in depth review of

---

16   Courts have a tremendous amount of documents to read each day. Your case is usu-
      ally one of several the court must deal with. Some of the cases will be postponed
      or "continued" at the last minute. Some courts get frustrated after spending their
      valuable time reading the case documents only to find that the matter has to be
      postponed or "continued" to a later date. Many courts will read over the papers filed
      by each side once they know the case is going forward.

your temporary orders request. It's not his or her fault. It is simply a crowded court system.

Don't despair, however, for there is a better way. Later I will present a better solution that will save both your patience and your pocketbook.

3. THE DISCOVERY PROCESS

The next destination on the family law roadmap is discovery, whereby each spouse has the opportunity to obtain evidence and information from the other side, in preparation for eventual settlement or trial. There are almost always significant facts in dispute. For example, what is the earning capacity of one or both spouses? Is the self-employed spouse making more money than is reflected in his or her tax return? What is the value of the community property portion of the spouse's business? You might need information from your spouse to achieve the custodial arrangement you consider best for the children.

Both sides will typically send out form interrogatories, which are written questions for the other party to answer in writing. Along with that, each side will demand that the other party produce documents such as tax returns, bank statements, insurance policies, and other documents the other side deems relevant. After documents have been exchanged, one or both parties may choose to ask the other party questions in a formal deposition. Another part of discovery is hiring experts who can attest to disputed matters, including forensic accountants or child custody evaluators. This can help determine the parenting plan, which would best serve the minor children.

Completing the discovery process can take six to nine months after the initial temporary orders hearing. It could take a year to wrap up discovery and the expert's work. Thousands and thousands of dollars have likely been spent, and we aren't even to the trial yet. In my experience, the discovery stage of the roadmap is where great abuses can occur and where the most money is wasted. Smart clients do what is only absolutely necessary.

3A. DECLARATIONS OF DISCLOSURE

Preliminary declaration of disclosure

An important part of the discovery process is each side's full disclosure of financial information. Within 45 days of the beginning of the case each side is required to provide the other with full disclosure of all assets and liabilities, as well as income and expenses. The initial disclosure statement is called the preliminary declaration of disclosure. The preliminary declaration should be as complete and have as much supporting documentation attached as possible. These disclosure statements serve as the basis for the other party's financial discovery. Each party must fully disclose his or her assets, liabilities, income and monthly expenses.

As the case progresses, each party must prepare a final declaration of disclosure, which must be served on the other spouse at least 45 days prior to trial. This disclosure statement must include even greater amounts of supporting documentation. If the parties are satisfied that the other party has provided sufficient disclosure in their preliminary declaration, the parties may waive service of the final declaration of disclosure.

Fiduciary duty

Spouses are deemed by law to have a "fiduciary duty" to each other. The law imposes on each spouse the highest duty of good faith and fair dealing to the marital partnership and the other spouse. This is a big area in family law, and the cause of much litigation and conflict.

One classic way for a spouse to breach a fiduciary duty to the other spouse is to not include an asset or liability on his or her disclosure statement. In one well-known case several years ago, a wife won a million dollars playing the lottery. The wife did not tell her husband that she had won the lottery. She then divorced him and failed to include her lottery winnings on her declaration of disclosure. After the divorce was final, the husband became aware of her lottery winnings. He hired an attorney and took his wife back to court, claiming that by fraudulently not disclosing her lottery winnings, she breached her fiduciary duty to him. The court agreed with the husband, and ordered the wife to pay not just half of her winnings (what the husband was originally entitled to as her spouse), but all of her lottery winnings to him as a penalty.

4. THE LAW AND MOTION PROCESS

As the case proceeds, the attorneys will at times need to get court rulings on matters they do not agree on. To do this, attorneys file motions, which consist of written declarations and case and statutory law that supports their requests. These matters are normally heard on Friday. Often the courts will issue tentative rulings on the court website the night before. Then the attorneys know what the judge is thinking and how he or she plans to rule. This allows them to go to the court next day prepared to argue their points.

Law and motion matters can be filed throughout the case, usually up to 15 days before trial. Clients are not required to attend these hearings, as the testimony of witnesses is not heard.

The law and motion process is an important part of the case where often crucial points are decided. The family law litigant can spend a lot of money with this process. It is important for spouses to be involved in the case and understand these motions.

5. TRIAL SETTING CONFERENCE

Once discovery is completed, the matter is considered "at issue," meaning it is ready for trial. One or both attorneys file a document with the court that indicates that the matter is ready for trial and gives the estimated length of the trial. The court then mails both sides the date of the trial setting conference, at which both attorneys must appear. Trial setting conferences are usually held within two months after the attorneys notify the court that the matter is ready for trial.

At the trial setting conference, the attorneys appear (usually without their clients) in court and verify that parties have served on the other their declarations of disclosure (which will be discussed in another chapter). Unless either side objects, the court will then order each side to attend the mandatory settlement conference, usually set for hearing 45 to 60 days later.

6. MANDATORY SETTLEMENT CONFERENCE

The mandatory settlement conference is another opportunity for both spouses and their attorneys to meet together and attempt to settle the case. By this time the discovery has usually been completed. The parties have exchanged disclosure statements and are now encouraged to attempt to settle the case before trial. In Orange County where I practice, mandatory settlement conferences are very informal. Both sides meet, usually in a nearby cafeteria, where they determine which issues can be settled. If both sides are willing to compromise either in whole or partially, the case can be resolved at this stage and the parties sign a handwritten agreement or a stipulation. This agreement will be formalized, signed by the court, and will become part of the judgment of dissolution of marriage.

In some counties, courts have a more effective mandatory settlement conference system. Third parties (often practicing family law attorneys) volunteer their time to help other attorneys and their clients settle their cases.

In the event the case does not settle, the court may order the parties to return on another day to attempt to settle the case again.[17] Or the court may set the matter for trial. Depending on the estimated length of the trial, the availability of the attorneys for both sides, and the court's own calendar, the hearing can be set anywhere from a few weeks to several months away.

---

17   The court will determine after speaking to the attorneys if the matter can likely be partially or fully settled. If the court thinks that settlement is promising more settlement conferences will be ordered. This can get out of hand and be a real money drain. One client that recently hired me had been to eight (8) mandatory settlement conferences and the case was still not resolved. If the case is not making real progress towards settlement, it needs to be set for trial. Or better yet it should first go to mediation with the supervision of a third party such as a retired judge. I will discuss this option later in this book.

If your case is going to trial, your attorney will need to do a considerable amount of additional work. Trial preparation is considerably more time intensive and difficult than settlement conference preparation. Information needs to be organized in a way that will be admissible as evidence. Subpoenas may need to be sent to financial institutions for authentic documents so they can be admitted into evidence at trial. Depositions of experts may be taken, at considerable cost. The parties may need to be deposed. Exhibits need to be organized and trial notebooks need to be prepared.

7. TRIAL

Trial is the process of presenting evidence and arguments to the court on the unresolved issues of the case. It is a formal event and the stakes are very high. Your attorney must be well organized and prepared.

When the day for your trial finally comes, you will arrive at court early and sit in the audience with your attorney. You may have hired experts to testify whom are also there or waiting on call to appear when your attorney calls them. On the court's calendar are several other cases the judge will attempt to resolve to move to your trial, which is the "main event." Some of the earlier cases can take a bit longer but by mid-morning the court has usually cleared his/her calendar and taken a mid-morning break. Then and only then your case will be heard. The court adjourns for his or her midmorning break. Usually by around 10:50 a.m. the judge resumes the bench and your trial begins. After a few preliminary matters, each of the attorneys gives their opening statement. The first witness is called, which is usually the petitioner, and he or she begins to testify. Then the court adjourns for lunch, and any witness testimonies that weren't completed continue after lunch.

Parties and counsel are ordered back by 1:30 p.m., the court takes the bench at 1:45 p.m., and the trial resumes. At approximately 3:00 p.m., the court takes an afternoon break. The courtroom is locked and you have the opportunity to use the restroom and speak with your attorney. By 3:20 p.m. the court has reopened and your trial is back in session until 4:30 p.m. If you've been adding up the time correctly, for the entire day in court, the actual trial time with the judge's full attention has been about three hours and 15 minutes. Meanwhile, your attorney has had to charge you for full-eight or-nine hours.[18] This doesn't

---

18 Some attorneys charge ten hours for a day of trial because of the demands of a day of trial which is typically preparation before the trial and follow up and continued follow up preparation for the next day of trial. This preparation is needed and extremely valuable. Attorneys meet their clients after trial to go over the testimony that has just been given to make needed adjustments for the next days' trial presentation as well as to consider additional rebuttal testimony. When attorneys are in trial, it is a day and night effort. If the trial is continued to a date days or weeks later, it is equally important to undergo the same process to assure the continuity of the presentation when the trial resumes.

include the additional preparation time your attorney may need to be prepared for tomorrow's day in court.

In my experience, trials tend to greatly exceed the time estimated to do them, usually for reasons that are out of anybody's control. This can result in the trial being pushed to another available time, which may be 30 to 60 days later. Because the judge will likely have had other trials and hearings in the interim, he or she will rely on the notes that (hopefully) were taken during the last trial session. Your attorney will also have to spend time gearing up for trial again.

Even worse, if your case involves financial issues only (such as child support, spousal support, or property division), it could get delayed again at the last minute. Courts give a higher priority to child custody and domestic violence matters, and so could delay your case if one of these matters needs attention.

Some judicial officers sensitive to this problem try hard to complete one trial before they start another trial. This benefits the people who are able to see their case resolved instead of postponed. But finishing one trial even if it exceeds the allotted time means that people who are ready for trial may have their court date "bumped" to a later date.[19] When this happens, it often happens at the very last minute and can be expensive and frustrating for the parties who were rescheduled.

---

19   The amount of time it takes to modify support payments is often frustrating for the party who believes he or she is overpaying child or spousal support.

Not infrequently, when the case finishes, the court will provide a ruling on one or more of your issues. That ruling can at times make you wonder if the judge fully understood your view of the case. That is just the reality of litigating in the highly crowded public court system. In short, going to trial, especially in the public court system is the most expensive and inefficient way to resolve your case.

Thankfully, as we will discuss in the next chapter, there is a more sensible way. Informed and wise litigants, who don't want to waste financial and emotional resources on attorneys and litigation can in most cases, shorten the litigation roadmap for a family law case considerably. These wise and informed people resolve their disputes while retaining more control of their lives, wasting fewer resources, enjoying greater personal satisfaction, and in most cases, better relationships with their ex-spouses.

chapter thirteen

Save Time and Money
Use a Private Judge

As discussed above, even the "typical" divorce case is a surefire way to strain yourself to the breaking point mentally, financially, etc.

Thankfully, good planning and decision-making can help you navigate the process more skillfully and will help you save time, heartache, and money. To help you prepare and navigate the process of winning a divorce case, you will need:

1. Meaningful Paid Consultation/Case Analysis with a Family Law Specialist

2. Initial filing of petition and response, and judge selection

3. Temporary (pendente lite) orders hearings

4. Discovery

5. Mediation with a Private Judge or Mediator

6. Trial with a private judge

Crucial step - mediation of the case with a private judge or mediator

The way to resolve most cases is to get the parties in front of a private judge or mediator as soon as possible. At least eighty-five percent (85%) of all cases will settle if the parties can agree to get their case to a private judge who can give some real attention to it early on in the process. If the parties and their attorneys can just agree to have their case assigned to a private judge or mediator they will find in the end that they are both more satisfied with the results.

A private judge is typically a retired superior court judge who provides services to litigants who hire them. After working in the public court system often for over 20 years, Superior Court judges retire and offer their services in the private sector. These judicial officers are extremely experienced and have heard thousands of family law cases. And better yet, the attorneys likely are familiar with these judges. These private judges handle only a few cases at a time. They can give your case the attention it deserves.

The private judge has the time to become familiar with the case early on and can read all of the briefing the attorneys can provide. He or she can take all of the time needed to become familiar with the case. This includes meeting with the parties and listening them. The parties are given all of the time they need to explain their positions directly to the judge. Once the judge is briefed on the legal issues of the case and has had time to speak to the parties and fully hear them out, he or she then sits with parties and their attorneys and assists them in reaching a reasonable settlement.

Using a private judge has tremendous advantages. Rather than going to an often chilly and intimidating courthouse, instead meetings take place in a warm and comfortable office building. Each side sits with their attorney in a separate private conference room at a conference table where they are able to comfortably discuss their concerns. The judge is clearly familiar with the case having had the opportunity to carefully spend hours as necessary reading the case file. The private judge meets with the parties' attorneys separately. Each side is given time to discuss their position with the judge who goes back and forth between the parties' conference rooms. Food is available throughout the day including snacks, drinks, and meals as needed.

While using a private judge does cost additional money, in the end it saves a far more than it costs. To complete your case in public system requires several court appearances by you and your counsel that will not be required if a private judge is hired early on. In the end it is really very economical as the case is brought to resolution so much faster. The financial investment ends up being less. The emotional cost is also less as once the case has been resolved you can move on toward greater healing.

My clients have experienced tremendous success using private judges. I have had cases settle early on that I thought had very little chance of settlement. These private judges are very experienced and have a tremendous amount of gravitas. When they speak people listen. It is a great experience for a client to be able to speak to the person that will decide their case and to feel and know that they are being listened to early on. Once both parties have been fully heard, albeit informally, the settlement process can really move forward.

I had a case not too long ago that involved a couple that had been married for approximately 25 years. This was a highly emotional case. Both spouses accused the other of being unfaithful. Both sides had already each fired at least one of their attorneys. The case had been going on for over three years. By this time the judge assigned to it was transferred to another branch of the court. This was truly a high conflict case. It was very difficult to get sufficient time for the assigned court to hear the case because it was so crowded. Finally, our case was given a trial date by the new court. Then just a few days before trial the opposing party terminated the services of her attorney. When we went to court on the trial day the new attorney for the opposing party requested a continuance and time to prepare as he was new on the case and needed time to get up to speed. The next available date for trial was not until six months later. I spoke to the new attorney for the wife and convinced him to try to mediate the case with a private judge. He agreed as long as my client would agree to advance the extra cost. With some convincing my client agreed to advance the funds to pay for the private judge.

Eight weeks later we met with a private judge both the parties and their attorneys agreed to. The meeting started at 1 o'clock. The private judge had read both of our briefs. As my client and I waited in one conference room the judge spoke to the other side for at least an hour. Then he came over to our side and my client and I were able to answers the judge's questions and concerns that he had just heard from the other side.

We were then able to present my clients side of the case. That day we made a partial settlement and agreed to come back two weeks later. Two weeks later we came back and spent the entire day and beyond going till about 7:30 that evening. But we left with a full resolution of the case fully written out and signed by both parties. It was the case that I had great doubts would ever settle without a trial. It seemed like a case that would go on forever. Yet, with the help and expertise of a private judge and the parties being able to fully be heard even this matter was resolved. It was a great blessing for each of these people to go on with their lives having this litigation behind them.

More common is the lower conflict case where the parties have some disagreements but just need closure. These cases are frequently resolved in one or two half-day hearings with the private judge.

The judges in the public court system could do the same thing if the system allowed them to do that. But it does not. The public court system assumes that the judges will try each case until such time as the matter is heard or settled.

chapter fourteen

Know When to Settle

"Better to yield when it is folly to resist, than to resist stubbornly and be destroyed."

— Aesop's Fables

Even though settlement means compromising, it's something you should look forward to. It marks the end of your legal battle, and a new chapter of your life. It's a fresh start. You aren't racking up attorney fees anymore, and you aren't stressing about the next date on the court calendar. It will be your time to move on from the past and build a new life.

Compromising means giving way on some demands so that you can be met on others. To settle the right way, be assertive to get what you need, yet yield on other things. It's a delicate balance, and every situation is unique. Here are some things to consider as you contemplate when it is time to settle:

1. Listen to your gut. You know the facts of your case and yourself best. What are your instincts telling you?

2. What is your attorney telling you? The relationship between you and your attorney should be one of complete trust. Try to hire a certified family law specialist and or one who is experienced and qualified to advise you on settlement. If your trusted and qualified attorney advises you to agree to a proposed settlement, that's a very reliable indicator that it would be wise to do so.

3. Is your attorney telling you to not to settle? In this case, consider it carefully. They should have concrete reasons (and not just his or her "gut feeling") why further litigation is in your best interest. If not, proceed with caution. Hopefully, your attorney is trustworthy and ethical. Drawn out litigation is one way attorneys make money. Only you can decide whether you want to keep funding ongoing litigation.

4. Do you totally trust your attorney's recommendations to settle? If not, it may be wise to quietly seek out a second opinion. Find another family

law specialist, pay for his or her time, and review the facts of the case and the proposed settlement.

5. What is the impact of the proposed settlement on your ability to parent and nurture your relationships with your children? Do you have a parenting plan that allows you the time you need with your children?

6. Do the proposed support orders allow you to meet your and your children's needs? Splitting one household into two (without raising income) affects the lifestyle you are probably used to living. Look at your finances and the proposed settlement and decide if it's something you can live with. If you're reasonably happy with things, that's a good sign.

7. What are the consequences of rejecting the proposed settlement? How much longer can you (or your ex) continue to bankroll an ongoing battle? Discuss with your attorney what would be the most likely (and other possible) outcomes from continued litigation.

8. Consider a private judge. Unlike judges working for the public court system, private judges have the time to truly review the facts of the case and confer with the parties. A meeting with a private

judge is likely to give you a better sense of whether settlement is right or not.

9. Have you reviewed the terms of the proposed settlement with an experienced family law trial attorney in your jurisdiction? Never in any circumstances sign any settlement paperwork without first having it reviewed by a qualified family law attorney. It's almost never appropriate for people to forego legal representation while they mediate, unless you have been married for less than a year with no children or shared assets. But nobody should ever sign any agreement until they have paid a family law specialist to review the proposed settlement.

At the end of the day, these are your kids, money and life. Only you can decide when settlement is right for you.

chapter fifteen
Work With Your Attorney

Try to choose an attorney who is easily reached. I give my clients my cell phone number for texts and calls. Other law practices make themselves available in other ways. I believe that a professional services provider should have his or her main phone answered during business hours. If a law practice cannot or will not have somebody available to answer phones during business hours, I wonder how they can provide the often times extensive amount of "hands on" help that is needed to protect a client and litigate a client's case.

Attorney-client privilege

A lawyer cannot divulge what a client tells him or her unless the client gives permission. This is called the "attorney-client privilege." It allows clients to communicate freely with their attorneys. And it allows attorneys to communicate freely with their clients about the strengths, weaknesses, strategies, and other aspects of a case.

This privilege is fragile and can be easily lost by a careless client. If anyone other than the client or his/her attorney is present during meetings, or communications between the client and the attorney are transmitted to someone else or are accessible by someone else, the privilege is likely to be broken. Often clients will want to bring their family or friends with them to their meetings with their attorney for "support." While moral support is a good thing having anyone else present when meeting with the attorney causes the attorney-client privilege to be lost.

Clients must also use caution when they use technology to communicate with their attorney. Many employers monitor internet usage and some even monitor the internet content of their employees' computers. Sending electronic communication that you know was monitored might endanger the privacy of your communication and therefore result in you losing the attorney-client privilege.

Be sure to discuss these topics with your attorney so that he/she can advise you on best practices. Our firm has a specific communications policy that we go over with our clients, and we use secure online services for sharing documents electronically.

Follow your attorney's counsel

There will be difficult times where you will not know what to do. Things happen that can be surprising or upsetting. You may get a settlement offer that you consider to be insulting or upsetting. You may view your judge as being unreasonably harsh to you. In these times, listen to your attorney and follow his or her counsel. Your attorney has likely been through divorce battles hundreds of times. Rely on his or her objectivity, especially in the hard moments.

Express appreciation when things go well

Be appreciative. Thank people who are working for you when something goes well. Call your doctor, accountant, attorney, or other service provider and show appreciation in even the smallest way when you feel well taken care of. Leave them a review online and let them know you did. They will truly appreciate it. Of course this is not necessary. After all, you are already paying for his or her services. However, when a client reaches out in even the smallest way and expresses appreciation for good work, it means so much. People remember and will work harder for you.

Be aggressive about your legal care

If you think that your law firm needs to emphasize something or are missing something, bring it to their attention. Communication is important. You know the facts of your case and your needs better than anyone. You may not have gone to law school, but you live your case 24 hours per day, seven days per week. If you feel something you are about to sign is not right, that a particular fact should be emphasized more, or that something could be made better, clarified, or improved, say so. Ultimately this is your case and your life. Be aggressive and speak up about what you want. It will pay great dividends.

chapter sixteen

Winning Your Trial

Although trial should be avoided if possible, some people will need to go to trial. Sometimes there are circumstances that defy compromise, such as when one spouse wants to move away with the children or when one spouse is mentally ill or has a personality disorder. These people are often confident that they can charm the judge, and have no intention of mediating in good faith. If you are confident that trial is truly unavoidable and mediation will be fruitless, consider going to trial as soon as possible rather than wasting resources and time in pointless mediation.

If you're going to trial, you want to win. Here are some points to consider:

1.   **Consider the cost**. You've got to count the cost before you go to trial. Take an honest, hard look at the situation. What's at stake? Are the potential wins

enough to truly justify the cost of trial? What would be lost if you settled on the other side's terms? Some things are priceless, like having your children in your life. Other things, like cars and homes, have specific monetary values. Count the cost so that you can be sure going to court is worth it.

2.   **Have the stronger team**. If you come to court with the weaker team, you are more likely to lose. Do a little digging and find out how experienced your ex's attorney is and compare your own legal team. How many years has each attorney practiced? How many people have they represented at trial? What does each attorney's support staff and legal team look like? If you don't have the winning team consider making some changes or reconsider going to trial.

3.   **Does your attorney interact well with the judge?** Your attorney should have good manners and not irritate the judge. If not, consider changing attorneys. Once during a hearing, I saw opposing counsel raise his hand to silence the judge. I could see the judge visibly bristle with anger at the disrespectfulness of the gesture. That is not the sort of attorney you want at your side during a trial.

4. **Get your documents in order as soon as possible.**
    You can't just use any document you print off as ev-
    idence in trial. Only documents that have been au-
    thenticated by the bank or other institution are ad-
    missible in court. Many family law trials have been
    won simply because one side was proactive about
    getting their documents in order early.

5. **Take time to prepare.** Preparing for trial takes time
    and money. There's no shortcut around the hard
    work that your legal team will need to do. If you've
    recently switched attorneys, you will need to give
    your new counsel time to prepare adequately.

6. **Does your spouse have more money?** If you are go-
    ing to trial when there is an imbalance of resources,
    ask for attorney's fees from the other side early and
    often.

chapter seventeen

Parentage
When You Are Not Married but Have Kids

More than one in three children in California are born to parents who are not married. The California family code has a separate section dealing with parentage or "paternity" cases. The law with regard to child custody, child support, and attorneys fees treats unmarried parents exactly the same as married parents. Parentage cases have their own set of legal forms. In some ways, because the court has more limited issues to rule on, parentage cases appear to be less complicated.

The determination of parentage and specifically who should be deemed to be the legal father of the child can get extremely complicated and intricate. In some cases, the mother is attempting to have the court determine that a certain man is the child's father. The court will almost always order any man named by the child's mother as a potential father to submit to a blood test to determine biological parentage. However, if the mother was married to another man at the time the child was conceived the mother's husband may still be deemed to be the father of the child with the biological father being excluded.

If you are in the situation of being married to the mother of a young child under three and you believe that the child is not yours, it is very important that you get a DNA test and file a challenge in court before the child is three years old. If the child is not your biological child you are still going to be presumed to be the biological father of the child unless you file suit against your spouse in family court for the purpose of rebutting the presumption.

There are many factual situations that give rise to different court decisions regarding paternity and parentage. This is a very intricate part of the law. If you are in this situation, get legal help from a competent and established family law specialist attorney as soon as you can.

chapter eighteen

Just When You Thought The Case Was Over:
Post Judgment Litigation

Family law judgments are unique in that many of them will need to be modified at some point. Children grow up and people remarry. Jobs are lost or changed. People relocate for employment or other circumstances. In these varied situations often the judgment you and your spouse arrived at perhaps years ago will need to be revisited.

In situations like this, the existing court orders may need modification. This is a significant area of family law. Nearly half of a family attorney's work involves clients who are seeking to modify an existing judgment.

Enforcing existing orders is another significant post judgment matter. This arises when one party fails to obey the judgment. This may involve a failure to abide by any number of provisions in the court order such as failing to pay financial obligations to the other spouse, or failing to return the children to the other parent in a timely fashion. In this case, the other party can file a motion for the court to do any number of things including sanctioning (fining) the offending party. The party seeking enforcement of the court order can also cite the offending person for contempt. A contempt proceeding is criminal or quasi-criminal in nature and can eventually result in the defending spouse serving jail time. However, if a spouse is found guilty of contempt the first punishment is typically a sentence of probation.

The advice found in this book applies fully to both parentage and post judgment matters.

chapter nineteen
Conclusion

Whether the case you are facing is dissolution of your marriage, a paternity/parentage matter, or a post judgment modification or enforcement, these issues can be complex. My hope is that this book gives you some insight on how to successfully navigate your way through the litigation process.

As state and county budgets become ever more strained, the problem of crowded courts will only increase. At the same time the law and the family court becomes increasingly complicated, and the conflict between spouses and potential co-parents seems to increase. This increased conflict creates a greater and greater demand for competent, compassionate, and caring attorneys who have the ability to bring a case to its logical conclusion as quickly as possible. The crowded and inefficient court system has resulted in a growth industry of retired judges and skilled mediators who can get cases settled.

Mediation with skilled attorneys and a neutral mediator can often abbreviate cases before the litigation costs spins out of control. This process can save families financially and lessen the emotional toll family law litigation takes on both parents and children.

Thank you for taking the time to read this book. I hope it has provided you with a greater understanding of the complexity of divorce and family law litigation. If you have questions about your individual situation, I encourage you to contact an experiened family law attorney in your area. If you are located in Orange County, CA, don't hesitate to contact my office through our website at **justfamilylaw.com** or by calling 949-363-5551.

About the Author

John A. Bledsoe has been practicing family law in Southern California since 1991. Prior to joining the legal profession, John was a corporate auditor for a major oil company.

John is the third oldest of 10 children, nine of whom are boys. He grew up in Southern California and served a two-year mission for his church in Iowa and Illinois. He married his wife Debra in 1982 and became the father of six children — five girls and one son. He has been married for the last 35 years. Of John's seven living brothers, three have law degrees and three have medical degrees.

John obtained his Bachelor's Degree in business administration from the University of Redlands. He then obtained a Masters Degree in finance from Golden Gate University. He then attended the night program at Western State University College of Law on an academic scholarship, graduating in 1991.

After passing the bar exam immediately after graduation, John started his own solo law practice where he gained considerable experience in the area of family law. In 2002, John was board certified by the State Bar of California as a Family Law Specialist. During his early years of being an attorney John also taught business law and other courses part time as an adjunct professor at the University of Phoenix.

In his limited spare time John enjoys working out, golfing, power walking, reading, traveling, shopping at Costco, cooking Sunday dinner for his family, and enjoying his children and young grandchildren. He feels very blessed to be in the legal profession and to have a great staff of professionals to work with each day.

Frequently Asked Questions

1. How long does it take to get divorced in California?

The hard and fast rule is it takes at least six months and one day from the date that summons and petition are served on the responding spouse. You simply cannot be divorced any faster than that even if your marriage only lasts a month or two. This does not mean that you will receive a decree of divorce automatically after six months and one day after having served your spouse the summons and petition or after you have been served with these documents. If you need to be divorced as soon as possible you will need to plan immediately for this. This includes getting your "ducks in a row" and complying with the applicable conditions of Family Code Section 2337, and filing a request also known as a motion with the Court to terminate your marital status before the other case issues are fully resolved.

This procedure that we refer to as a "Status Only Dissolution" is granted only with certain conditions. For instance, if the spouse who seeks the early marital status termination is the spouse that carries the medical insurance for the family that spouse must provide at his or her own cost a separate insurance policy for the other spouse who will not any longer be entitled to be covered under the family policy due to being divorced.

Unless special steps are taken to terminate the marital status, it will take at least a year to get divorced if you go through the normal series of hearings, discovery, trial setting and settlement conferences and trial. The courts are simply way too crowded.

2. What if I cannot afford to retain an attorney?

Most people do not have money available at the outset of commencing divorce litigation to retain counsel. Our firm is quite unique in that we have arranged access to **special financing** for our potential clients to apply with several different lenders who specialize in assisting parties with funds to litigate their cases. After a soft credit check, qualifying applicants will receive loan offers based on pre-qualification within seconds, and funds in your account in a few days. Even if you do not qualify for a personal loan, we have a monthly payment option through a third party lender as well. If you cannot afford an attorney there are ways to get the necessary funds. Nobody should ever automatically not attempt to access funds until they have consulted with an attorney for at least an hour. Even spending a modest amount of money on an attorney can pay substantial dividends. Having an attorney represent you for temporary support orders often result in the other side being ordered to contribute to what you pay your attorney.

3. What if we both make about the same amount of money and have no children to fight over or very modest property to divide?

In situations like this, mediation with a qualified mediator or attorney is also an excellent choice. If both spouses are willing to work together and can "put down their swords" they can often arrive at a complete resolution early in the process.

4. What effect has the recent COVID-19 pandemic had on the California family court system and how will that affect my ability to get a divorce?

All of the Superior Courts in Southern California closed in mid-March. As this book goes to print in mid-May 2020, the courts are just beginning to reopen. There is a huge backlog of work that needs to be completed for cases that are already in existence. And the stress brought by the pandemic has also resulted in a considerable amount of new domestic violence cases and divorce cases. It is expected that the courts will be extremely crowded for the foreseeable future. Criminal cases and domestic violence cases take priority over regular divorce cases. This further over crowding of the courts makes the advice in this book to seek other informal avenues of resolution even more timely and relevant.

5. How is child support in California determined?

Child support is based upon a number of factors that are included in a complex computer calculation that is based upon parameters set down by the California legislature. These calculations are done on very sophisticated computer programs with names like "Xspouse" or "Dissomaster" or "SupportTax." These factors include but are not limited to the net incomes of each of the parents, the amount of time the children are in the physical custody of the parents, the tax filing status of each of the parents and other important factors.

At a hearing where child support is ordered the Court will always have a desktop computer where he or she is calculating child support on one of these programs. The attorneys each argues as to what factors the court should input into the calculation. Courts are strongly encouraged by the legislature to order the amount of child support calculated by the support program. The Court then gives a printout of the calculation to each side. Courts rarely deviate from the "guideline amounts" issued by program results.

6. How is alimony (spousal support) determined?

When spouses initially separate and move apart from each other often one of them will seek spousal support from the other. In this situation, at the front end of the case the court will typically use one of the child support programs listed above to calculate temporary spousal support. The computer programs discussed above have an option to also calculate temporary spousal support.

As the case progresses and gets to the trial stage where a final judgment will be determined, courts do not use the

Child support programs to determine spousal support. Instead, each case is decided on an individual basis based upon factors the California legislature has listed under Family Code Section 4320. Each case is unique. The length of the marriage is a crucial factor. A marriage of less than ten (10) years in length is considered to be a short-term marriage and spousal support is usually awarded for only half of the length of the marriage. A marriage exceeding ten years in length is a long term marriage and spousal support is often ordered until the supported spouse dies or remarries.

Other important factors considered by the court under Family code section 4320 include the age, health, education, income, earning potential, and any special needs of each of the spouses. Also considered is whether or not a spouse gave up opportunity to earn, learn and progress in a career for the sake of the marriage and family. All of these factors make a spousal support case absolutely fascinating. At the same time, to one degree or another each spouse is expected to become self-supporting to the standard of living of the marriage as soon as practical.

Long-term spousal support is not highly favored by California public policy except in rare situations. Financial circumstances change and support orders can always be modified due to one or both sides have any change in income or loss of employment.

7. What if I have children with my partner but we were never married and now we are breaking up?

The California Family Code provides certain substantial protections for unmarried couples with minor children who are separating, living apart or who have never lived together. Parties with children are protected in that they can seek orders from the other pertaining to custody, visitation and support of children. Courts treat unmarried parties the same with regard to issues of child custody and child support as well as the need of one party to be awarded attorneys fees from the other due to a discrepancy between the partys' abilities to access funds to litigate these important issues.

Parentage issues are complex. As to the actual paternity of the child, the issues are much more complex to the point of being intricate. Always consult with an attorney early and often in this type of a case.

8. What is the one thing you would tell a person who is getting divorced and has not had the benefit of having an attorney?

I would tell anybody to do whatever is necessary to find the money to hire a family law specialist to review their proposed judgment before they sign it. Never settle a divorce or paternity dispute without getting the advice of a competent attorney who specializes in family law. Even an hour of time spent with the right attorney at the right time can provide amazing peace of mind and can prevent crucial mistakes from being made. Even if the other party shows up without an attorney, always assume that they are consulting with an attorney behind the scenes. Do whatever you need to do to be protected. An hour or two of consultation with a competent attorney at the beginning and end of your case will most certainly pay huge dividends. You simply cannot afford not to have good legal advice in what is a very complicated field.

Client Testimonials

"You know the term 'turn the tables?' We did it with Attorney Bledsoe. His fast and precise thinking and financial background served us exceptionally well. You know this desperate moment you "have been served" with court papers? He took my case even though it looked like a disaster - now it is pretty far from it. Much appreciated your efforts, Mr. Bledsoe!" -*O.K.*

❖❖❖

"Yesterday I was in court because when my wife and I separated she moved all of our property out of our home and took all liquid assets, well over six figures. I had a good day in court. She put on an outrageous and dramatic act with crying, making false and outrageous lies about me and attempted to manipulate the court. John Bledsoe insisted on a hearing and that she answer specific questions about what she did with our money that she took. John Bledsoe held my wife accountable. I was impressed on how carefully the Judge listened to John compared to my wife's attorney. When it was all over the Court ordered my wife to bring all of the money she had left and put in my attorney's trust account within 72 hours. The result of John's questioning of my wife was that she looked terrible to the Judge and ended up painting herself into a corner. She has found herself in big trouble. John Bledsoe really earned his money at court yesterday. If you're looking for the best attorney that understands the law, commands the courtroom and can be a bulldog when required, I would highly recommend John Bledsoe." -*J.G.*

***

"John, before the weekend gets underway....I just couldn't let today go by without taking the time to express to you my deep appreciation for seeing me through this entire difficult journey of mine.... every step of the way for years and especially for your role yesterday. For providing your tremendous support, sound guidance, legal expertise, excellent intuition, and for bringing your unique sensitivity to the matter at all times...and in all areas....I truly thank you John. Through it all.... I felt both proud and safe in having you as my attorney. It is your high integrity and standards, your honesty, your reliable character, and your consistent good nature that puts your clients at ease and provides a sense of security throughout the process.... even during times of frustration and uncertainty during the case - you remain calm and empathetic. And above all....it is your talents as a peacemaker that sets you apart from the rest. You fight for what is right for your client but in a constructive way. And that helps everyone in the process. Your gift is that you think about all of the players...how they might be feeling. And while you are representing one party....it doesn't preclude you from understanding where the opposing parties may be coming from. You consider all angles of the case....then proceed in a manner that is reasonable and fair.

So again JB, yesterday being as difficult as it was for me, was made a whole lot better just knowing you had my and N's best interests at heart and that in these difficult negotiations....you guarded and guided and protected your client. The only word that I can use to describe what I am feeling today is a total sense of RELIEF!! The peace that can now come to our home because of the settlement is priceless. My daughter and I have peace of mind in knowing that our home remains our home and that the school she loves attending remains her school. It is so HUGE for a young teenager to have this sense of security and for me too! YOU made it happen. You lead this case down a path that brought me here and I am grateful for this, for all you have done." –*M.M.*

❖❖❖

"John is a pro, and helped me every step of the way, earning more time with my daughter and getting a fair outcome for our family." –*S. V.*

✿✿✿

"John Bledsoe and his staff were always available to me. They handled my difficult case with strong ethics and morals. They were organized and John knew every detail of my crazy divorce. He always had a plan, yet listened and took into account my wants and plans. Thank you John and the rest of your staff." –*J.M.*

"Incredible attorney and a great experience with this law firm. John Bledsoe is very knowledgeable and always had my best interest in mind. He is somebody you can trust and I could not recommend him enough." –*N.B.*

✿✿✿

"John gave me some GREAT advice about my case. He's extremely accessible and knowledgeable about California family law. He knows all the local players. I highly recommend him and his staff." –*M.N.*

✿✿✿

"I was so impressed with John and how he handled my son's custody case. He was reassuring to my son who was beside himself. We prevailed in court. I can't thank John enough." - **D.V.**

✧✧✧

"Mr. John Bledsoe and his legal team are a cut above. John listened effectively and ascertains that you understand the strategy. He is a no-nonsense professional." - **L.B.**

✧✧✧

"John handled my divorce. He handled it so well that when my ex lost all of her initial motions that she filed she fired her attorney and got another one! It didn't help as John prevailed on everything. No spousal support and 50/50 custody. John answered all of my questions and gave good advice on what to do, how to do it, and how long it would take. Divorce is a horrible thing I hope you don't experience. But if you find yourself in that position, I recommend you use John Bledsoe." –**B.L.**

✧✧✧

"Walking into a courtroom with Mr. Bledsoe on your team immediately adds to your credibility. Whether or not you can maintain that credibility is on you and how well you heed his counsel. This is a 5 star law firm for those who can recognize the long term value of their representation. -**B.M.**

✿✿✿

"I was in a desperate situation with a controlling ex-husband who lived out of the country part-time and had convinced the judge that I should not be able to move to be near my family. My previous attorney had little success. Attorney Bledsoe came on the case. We had a trial. He was very strong and I could tell that the judge listened to him. John Bledsoe destroyed my ex on his cross-examination of him. The next thing I knew I was allowed to move with my children where I could be near to my extended family." -**B.N.**

✿✿✿

"Attorney Bledsoe was able to get my support payments from my ex-husband increased. He is an expert in the financial area. I am so pleased with the results."- **D.W.**

✿✿✿

"Attorney Bledsoe assisted us in getting custody of our granddaughter. She was with her birth parents and the situation was not where any child should be. Other attorneys had told us it would be almost impossible to get custody from birth parents. Attorney Bledsoe fought hard and really knew the law. He assured us that grandparents do have rights, especially when it is in the best interest of the child. We are so very grateful to John A. Bledsoe for all he did in getting us full custody of our granddaughter." –*J.M.*

❀❀❀

"John Bledsoe helped me negotiate my alimony settlement after my ex hired an attorney who said he loves working with guys like me. Her attorney was very aggressive and threw out some very large numbers and claimed I would be paying for his time as well. John helped me avoid that and I ended up paying less than half of what her attorney proposed." –*M.N.*

For additional client testimonials Google:
The Bledsoe Firm LLC

THE BLEDSOE FIRM

LAW OFFICES OF JOHN A. BLEDSOE

(949) 363-5551
www.justfamilylaw.com

WA